SO-EIE-312

Greetings!

Greetings!

How to make your own cards...
for birthdays, anniversaries, parties,
holidays, special days, any days

Peter and Maria Snow

Bobbs-Merrill
Indianapolis/New York

Published by The Bobbs-Merrill Company, Inc.
Indianapolis/New York

ISBN 0-672-52237-3 Hardcover

Library of Congress Catalog Card Number: 76-10083

Designed and produced by Walter Parrish International .Ltd
London

Designer Judy Tuke

Line drawings by Amaryllis May

Photographs taken by A. C. Cooper Ltd and
Colin Tait Studios, London

Printed and bound in Great Britain by Purnell & Sons Ltd.
First U.S. printing

Contents

Which to use when

The suggestions below are our own—you may have your own, different ideas. There are several designs in the book not listed here—these are very adaptable and can be used for almost any occasion. The numbers are page numbers. Where several designs are shown on one page, they are indicated by *a, b,* or *c,* starting from the top of the page.

Baby's birth   24*a,* 81*a,* 81*b*

Birthdays

    Child's   24*a,* 32*a,* 34 *(both),* 63*a,* 72*c,* 89*a,* 89*b*

    Teenager's   29*a,* 32*a,* 72 *(all),* 89*c*

    Twenty-first   29*a,* 32*a,* 60*b*

    Female adult   24*b,* 29*a,* 32*a*

    Male adult   29*a,* 30*a,* 30*b,* 32*a*

Engagement   24*a,* 32*b,* 60*d,* 68, 73*b,* 93*b*

Wedding   41*a,* 42*a,* 65*b,* 93*b*

Wedding anniversary   41*a,* 42*a,* 93*b*

Mother's Day   24*b,* 36*a,* 41*a*

Father's Day   30*a,* 92*b*

St. Valentine's Day   32*b*

Christmas   32*a,* 36*b,* 45*a,* 45*c,* 50*b,* 65*b,* 67*a,* 69, 70, 81*b,* 81*c,* 88 *(both)*

Introduction

We have written this book to help you make festive occasions and holidays even more special. We all like sending cards to our relations and friends, and the pleasure of giving and receiving is infinitely greater when the card itself is a really individual creation.

Commercial products are not the answer. It is certainly true that there is no lack of cards on sale in the stores, and sometimes we have found the sheer numbers of apparently varied designs positively daunting. And yet, when it actually comes to choosing something for a relative, a friend or even each other, looking for that elusive quality which shows we are thinking of one particular person, the selection somehow evaporates, and we are left with one or two unoriginal or garishly comic choices. Recently, one Christmas, seven different people sent us the identical printed card, a sharp reminder of how mass production and commercialisation have sadly devalued an expression of personal affection and seasonal goodwill.

Of course, it is good to be remembered in any way at all, and we would not pretend otherwise. But it is so much more meaningful if the card itself is part of your message—a unique way of sharing happiness, a visible expression of friendship and love. We always look forward with extra delight to the cards made or painted by our friends, whether they are artists or accountants. Children, too, love to make pictures full of imagination. We treasure all of these, because the simple fact that someone has taken such trouble to produce something just for us makes the occasion very special. Some we even frame, so that the pleasure outlives the day and become a permanent delight.

Recently, it has seemed that many other people have come to feel the same way, and would like to make their own cards. So how do you go about it? This is what the book is all about. What is needed is practical advice, help and encouragement—and we hope that we have provided it here. The ideas and techniques illustrated are more than just models for you to copy. They should also stimulate your own

A decorative example of a design using the scraper-board technique, which is simple and effective, and gives a very 'professional' finish.

9

powers of creativity. It is amazing what you can do when you try—with the simplest of materials, and often at great savings in cost, you can have the satisfaction of sending something personal and distinctive to your family and friends. And, too, you will be able to use the methods shown in all sorts of ways—we suggest some at the end of the book; but, really, there is no limit to the permutations of design and indeed the broader range of applications—stencilled furniture, painted T-shirts, needlework, party decorations.

In short, this whole book is our greetings card to you.

How to use the book

This book is arranged so that a number of different techniques for producing cards are dealt with in turn. They are illustrated with our own designs, which you may take as basic patterns—but you can also develop the patterns yourself in all sorts of ways. They may be decorated with your own choice of colours, textures and motifs, they can be made simpler or more complicated, combined with one another and so on. We hope they will inspire you to make many other designs of your own.

The first thing to do, once you have decided what kind of card you are going to produce, is to gather the necessary materials together. In the instructions for each technique the materials needed are listed. Before you start, it is well worth reading the section starting on page 13, where the types of material are briefly discussed in turn. None of the things we have used are out of the ordinary, and they should all be readily available from an art store, or in many cases a stationer's. In many instances you will be able to improvise—for example, you don't really need a proper drawing-board; a large bread-board can be used instead. But you will need the right implements for lino-cutting, or producing scraper-board designs, which are easily bought and not particularly expensive.

The different techniques used are all quite simple. They are stencil-cutting, collage, potato-cut, lino-cut, tracing, scraper-board, ink blot, cut-out, silhouette, and the use of combinations of these, which we have grouped under the heading 'Mixed Media'. In most of the sections there are coloured illustrations of some finished cards, and general, step-by-step instructions for the technique. Where necessary, there are line drawings to make the instructions absolutely clear. We have also added helpful hints where necessary—the sort of thing you only discover once you have actually tried to make something, and it has gone wrong.

Many of today's traditional symbols, such as bells for the New Year and weddings, holly for Christmas, hearts for St

Valentine's Day, and the ancient menorah lamp of the Israelites to celebrate Hanukkah, are of long standing; they convey a particular meaning that people have come to associate with special occasions over a long period of time. Many artists, for thousands of years, have used traditional patterns and symbols which they have incorporated into their own designs, and these have often been the inspiration for great creative activities in many fields. The ancient Egyptians, Romans and Greeks, for example, started from extant visual material, motifs of flowers, fruit, animals, fish, birds, and images of their gods and goddesses, using these in decorative forms in their paintings, books, architecture and tombs.

There are many celebrations in our year for which we can invent our own symbols—such as birthdays, Mother's and Father's Days, and so on. For these, you can allow yourself great freedom in the choice of subject. For instance, if you know that the recipient of the card is interested in music, sport, art, gardening, travelling, or some other pastime, you could incorporate some pictorial motif associated with any of these. One of the great attractions in freeing yourself from what is commercially available is that you can get away from the predictable and the stereotyped. You will find in the book ideas to use as a starting-off point for many specific occasions in the year, and at the beginning there is a list, arranged occasion by occasion, which shows you where to find them. A design idea in the stencil section, for example, can often be perfectly well used as a paper cut-out, and so on.

Because each design may be suitable for treatment in more than one medium, beside each drawing are symbols to show which forms of treatment we feel is best—so that you can see at a glance how, for example, a design in the stencil section might be treated in different ways, perhaps as a lino-cut, as a traced card or as a cut-out. The symbols for each technique are shown on the right.

On page 97 are some hints to show you how particular motifs can be adapted for treatment in different media. To help you use the designs in the book as patterns to be followed exactly, if this is the approach you prefer, there are directions on page 98 for making a design bigger or smaller.

The instructions for each technique tell you how to produce the design itself—it is, of course, very important to present your finished card well, by mounting the design neatly, and getting the overall proportions of the card right. Under 'Materials' we discuss the different sorts of background materials you can use, and on page 101 are further hints on mounting and trimming designs. If you want to include a message on your cards by some means other than handwriting, we touch briefly on methods for doing this on page 102.

Key to symbols

 stencil

 collage

 potato-cut

 lino-cut

 scraper-board

 tracing and colouring

 blots

 cut-out
folding and cutting

 silhouette

11

Whatever the form of the card, it must eventually fit into an envelope if it is to be sent in the mail. You may therefore have to design it to fit a standard envelope size, in which case you must remember to make it slightly smaller than the envelope itself.

Some typical sizes for envelopes in the UK and USA are given below.

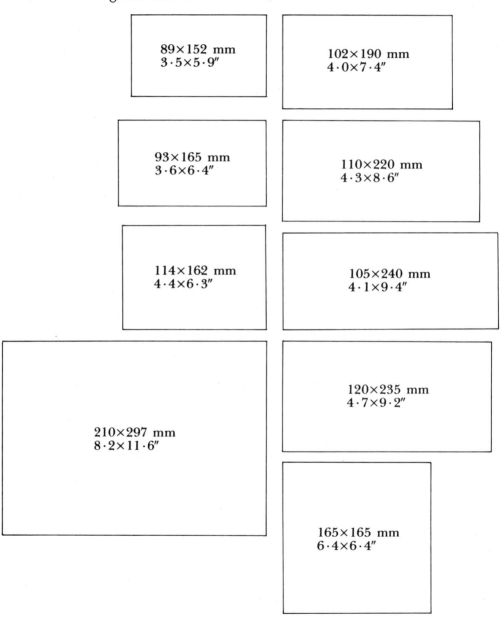

On page 102 are instructions for making envelopes for your cards which do not fit these sizes. Any envelopes sent through the mail will have to fit into a letter-box, so there will always have to be some limitation as to size.

Some of the cards are particularly suitable for occasions which would probably only call for a single, 'one-off' card, such as a birthday or a wedding—in these cases you will probably be able to take longer over them than those which need to be produced in batches—say for Christmas and New Year, or invitations to parties.

Where you do need a batch of cards, you will find that the initial preparation may take as long as it would in the design of the individual cards, but then certain methods such as lino-cut and potato-cut allow you to reproduce them as many times as you need, speedily and effectively. It is, of course, possible even in these cases to ring the changes on the colour, so that although the basic design is the same, there is an element of variety in the results. It is surprising how a different colour combination can alter the feeling and character of the design, and there is no reason at all why producing batches of cards should seem repetitive. Introducing new colours will also make the creative process more interesting, enjoyable and experimental for yourself.

Then, too, it could be great fun for other members of your family, or friends, to join together in a co-operative art activity and to help in making a number of cards. Working within a basic design, they would be free nevertheless to interpret their own ideas of colour and texture, and the results will be lively, original, and often surprising!

Materials

This is a general guide to all the materials we mention. Of course, you will not need them all for every card, and in the section on each method there is a list of requirements for that particular one. The materials are, for the most part, inexpensive and easily obtained at art shops, stationery shops and department stores. You will not need complicated, expensive, very messy or specialised printing processes, so that the work may be done quite simply at home.

The base card

The card itself will need to be made from a sheet of white or coloured cardboard. This should be no thicker than two or three postcards, so that it can fit easily into a standard envelope.

It is more convenient if you are able to use a base which is already coloured, if you are making a card with a coloured background, to save having to colour it yourself. This way you also get a more even background colour. However, if you find the choice is too limiting, then one way round the problem is to cover the basic material with some coloured paper, which will need to be glued on—this will give an all-over matt or shiny appearance, and looks more neat and efficient than if it were painted with a brush. Most good art suppliers stock a selection of coloured papers, and it is a good idea to buy a number of these at a time.

It is also possible, of course, to obtain water-based paints in spray cans, usually from shops which supply materials for commercial art studios, but these are expensive and hardly worth while unless you are making batches of cards.

In some cases you will need to print your card onto a piece of paper, and then glue the paper onto the base card. For potato-cuts and lino-cuts, for example, the best paper to print on is absorbent—you can even use blotting-paper. Japanese rice paper is specially recommended. It is easily available in rolls or sheets from stores specialising in Oriental products, and elsewhere.

For cutting your stencils, the best material to use is waxed or parchment card. The waxed surface prevents the paint being absorbed, and so helps to give a clean-cut effect to the stencil.

Glues and pastes

One of the best glues to use is a rubber- and petroleum-based one. Products of this kind can be purchased in a large tube or in a can, and may be spread on evenly with a specially provided plastic spreader. This type of adhesive has one great advantage: when it is dry, any residue left on the card may be easily rubbed away, so that you have no messy, sticky bits left visible. A paste in a bottle is also suitable, and this you can apply with the brush often provided. You will have to be more careful when using this—only the actual areas which need to be pasted must be covered.

Spray-gun glue is also excellent, although this is expensive and is impossible to remove should you make any mistakes. It is necessary, when using it, to place a mask on the card, exposing only the area you wish to stick, so that the glue is confined exactly to the area you want. On the other hand, you can apply it very evenly, and this is particularly important if you are using thin or metallic paper, where lumps tend to show. A transparent quick-drying glue in a small tube is recommended for sticking on sequins, feathers, etc. Impact adhesive is useful for sticking lino onto a cardboard base, when you are doing lino-cuts.

Cutting tools

It is useful to have two pairs of scissors, of different sizes. These *must* be kept sharpened. A knife or surgical scalpel with disposable blades is another essential. These may be bought from an art store or a supplier of carpenter's tools, as may also a steel-edged rule; you can use the two together to trim your cards. Specialised lino-cutting tools may be purchased at an art store. These are bought in kits, and consist of a wooden holder into which various alternative blades may be fitted (you can also buy the components in the kit separately complete with handle). In conjunction with the cutting tool, you will need a special roller for applying the ink to the lino, and a thick piece of glass or some similar material to roll the ink out on. You can use the same handle as part of your scraper-board kit, with a different set of blades.

A table- or kitchen-knife may be used for cutting potatoes into two, when you are doing cuts, but for cutting out the pattern a scalpel or trimming-knife is better.

lino-cut and scraper-board tools with fixed blades

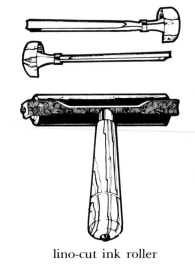

lino-cut holder with inter-changeable blade

scissors

disposable trimming knife

safety razor blade

stencil brush

lino-cut ink roller

Mark-makers and paints

Paint-brushes can be bought in any art store. These sometimes seem expensive, and it is a temptation to economise here—but don't. It is not worth buying cheap ones, which soon deteriorate and fall to bits. Buy sable brushes if you can, and you will probably need three sizes—large (sizes numbered 6–8), medium (4–5) and small (1–3).

You can also buy brushes specially intended for stencils—instead of the bristles graduated in length so that they come to a point, they are short and stubby. You will need two, of different sizes. You can also use any stubby hog's-hair brush for stencils.

In order to make guide-line marks, you will need an HB pencil. This must be kept sharp in order to draw out the card itself, and indicate where the pattern is to occur. If you are using carbon paper to trace the pattern onto your card or onto lino or scraper-board, use an H pencil (which is harder than an HB) or a ballpoint pen.

Coloured pencils may be bought individually or in sets, and it is advisable to purchase a reputable brand, as otherwise the coloured leads break in the wood and they cannot be sharpened properly. The effect given by the best

spare scalpel blades

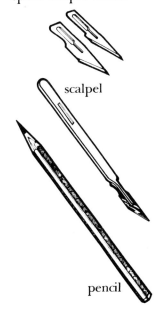

scalpel

pencil

brands is generally clear and shiny, like coloured china, and the results tend to be rather attractively subtle and muted, particularly in the paler colours.

Crayons or oil pastels tend to have more body than pencils, and make denser marks, though, because they cannot easily be sharpened to as fine a point as the pencils, they should be kept for larger, bolder areas of colour. The crayons themselves may be of the type that children use, mostly in brilliant colours, or of an oil-based type which may be smudged with a little white spirit on cotton wool. There is a large selection on the market made by Japanese, British and American firms.

Chalk pastels are also available. These are best used on paper or card which has a slightly textured surface. They will need to be sprayed afterwards with some fixative, either from an aerosol can or by using a spray tube dipped into a bottle of fixative.

Felt pens also make brilliant marks, and there is a large selection of these now available, in different sizes and shapes, from pencil-thin to very broad. The marks they make are transparent, rather like ink.

Ink itself may be purchased in bottles, and may be diluted with water if it is too strong in colour. Ink can be used in the same way as paint, and gives a beautiful translucent quality, rather like stained glass.

For lino-cuts you will need printing-ink, which can be bought in various colours. It can be bought in tubes; if you require a large amount, it is best bought in cans or plastic containers. Water-based brands are more easily removed in case of accidents, perhaps with a little washing-up liquid; if you are using an oil-based ink, white spirit will remove it.

Paints should all be water-based. The best types for our purposes are 'designers' colour', 'gouache', or 'poster-colour'. They all have their own particular properties. Designers' colour is the most expensive. It comes in tubes, and can be bought in a wide range of colours. It gives a transparent effect, almost like water-colour. Gouache is slightly less expensive, and also comes in tubes in a wide range of colours. It has a little more body than designers' colour, and gives a less transparent effect. Poster-colour is the cheapest of the three, and comes in little bottles. It is rather more restricted in its colour range, but is excellent for bold designs.

Water-colour can also be used, but this is a deceptively different medium. It has less body even than designers' colour and you really need a very good paper to achieve good results.

In conjunction with the paint you will also need a jar of water to clean the brushes in; paper plates are very useful for mixing colours on.

Erasers, pins and adhesive tapes

Soft art gum erasers are recommended for getting rid of pencil marks and any other marks which disfigure your designs.

Drawing-pins (thumb-tacks) can be purchased at your local stationery store, as can transparent self-adhesive tape. These are useful for fixing your card in position on the drawing-board while you are working on it—particularly important if you are tracing a design through. Even better than transparent tape, if you want to stick down your card without producing pin holes, is masking tape, which is generally used by house-painters and decorators (and may be bought in stores where house-painting equipment is sold, as well as in some art stores); it is generally easier to remove than the transparent tape, which sometimes tears paper or card.

Drawing-boards

You will need a board of some sort on which to pin or stick your designs while working on them. You can buy drawing-boards specially made for artists—you will only need the smaller size. It is perfectly possible to improvise a drawing-board, making do with a pastry-board or a bread-board as a base.

Tracing-paper and carbon paper

Tracing-paper is necessary for transferring a design onto your cards from the line drawings in the book or from any other source. It may be bought in single sheets or in book form. Carbon paper is sold in packets and may be blue, rust-coloured or black.

Collage materials

Collage materials are coloured papers which may be bought from your art store. They may be plain, textured, metallic, or printed with some kinds of pattern—you can use many everyday materials as well, such as wallpaper or wrapping-paper. You can also cut out a variety of printed matter from magazines and the like.

In the category of collage materials we would also include sequins, feathers, sand, glitter, seeds, and any other material which may be glued onto the card to form an interesting tactile pattern. Cards can have variations in texture as well as in colour. Many collage materials can be collected in the home over a period of some weeks in preparation for your card-making. No doubt you will be able to find novel materials of your own with which to make an inventive and original surface. Make sure, however, that whatever you use remains stuck firmly onto your card, is not too heavy or bulky, and is not in danger of falling off in the mail . . . you do not want your cards to arrive in bits!

Stencil

Stencils are patterns which are cut out with a knife from parchment paper or waxed card. The cut-out image is then stippled with a suitable brush, or marked through the holes with some other suitable mark-maker, leaving a clear, sharp image on the paper or card underneath.

Some designs are more suitable for stencil treatment than others—bold, decorative, flat drawings are best adapted, and this can be done quite easily. Remember that in order for the stencil to hold together physically, the cut-out areas must often be broken with bridges, links of parchment card, which give almost a spider's-web effect. The stencil structure thus becomes part of the design, and this is what gives stencilled cards their characteristic decorative quality. Stencils may be complicated and fragile, like those made by the Japanese in printing their sophisticated, beautiful fabrics—however, simple, bold patterns of the kind used in wallpaper designs and book jackets are just as effective, especially for greetings cards.

Once it has been made, one stencil can be used many times if you take reasonable care, and so one design can be repeated with variations in colour on white or coloured card. Stencils are ideal for producing cards in batches. They are therefore particularly good for invitations, or Christmas cards, and for general cards which may be kept in reserve and used for any celebration where a traditional symbol is not required.

Materials

Drawing-board
Tracing-paper
Adhesive tape or drawing-pins
  (thumb-tacks)
Pencil (HB)
Waxed or parchment card
Carbon paper
Pencil (H) or ballpoint pen
Trimming-knife or scalpel

White or coloured card or paper
Poster or gouache colours
Water jar
Stencil brush
Paper plates for mixing colours

What to do

1. Put the pattern to be adapted on your table or drawing-board, facing upwards.

2. Place the tracing-paper over the pattern, and fix it with tape or drawing-pins so that it does not slip while you are tracing.

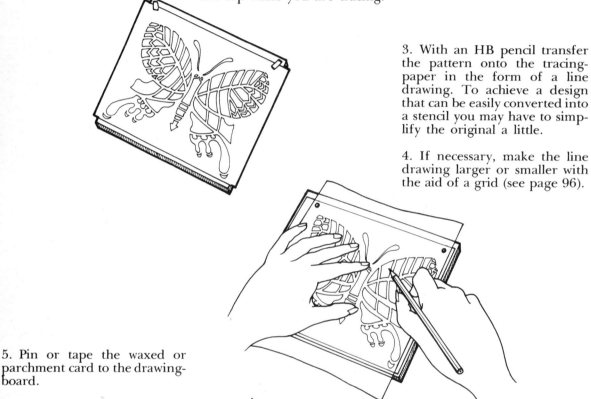

3. With an HB pencil transfer the pattern onto the tracing-paper in the form of a line drawing. To achieve a design that can be easily converted into a stencil you may have to simplify the original a little.

4. If necessary, make the line drawing larger or smaller with the aid of a grid (see page 96).

5. Pin or tape the waxed or parchment card to the drawing-board.

6. Cover it with a sheet of carbon paper, carbon side down.

7. Put the tracing-paper with the pattern on it over the carbon paper, taping or pinning it down at the corners so that it does not slip.

8. With an H pencil or ballpoint pen trace over the lines, imprinting them through the carbon paper onto the parchment paper.

9. When the pattern has been completely transferred to the parchment, take away the tracing-paper and carbon paper. The image is ready for cutting out.

 *Stencil*

10. Shade or colour the areas on the stencil you intend to cut out, so that in the event you do not cut away the wrong pieces—it is an easy thing to do! Make sure you have left bridges in the right places, so that pieces don't fall out of your pattern. The areas to be cut out are shaded on the design diagrams later in this chapter.

11. Carefully cut out the pattern with a knife.

12. Take the parchment off the board, and pin or tape down the card or paper on which you are going to print the design. It is a good idea to allow about an inch of paper all round the actual area of the card—this can be trimmed away afterwards. Then, if you pin this down, the marks will not show on the finished card.

13. Place the stencil over the card and fix this, too, firmly down.

14. Mix up the colours you need—they should be like thick cream in consistency. If they are too dry and sticky they will not brush on easily, and if they are too wet they will leak under the edge of the parchment and make unsightly blotches. Practise beforehand on some spare pieces of paper, as this will help you to find out the right consistency of paint.

15. Take a brush full of colour and stipple it through the cut-out pattern. It is better not to use more than two or three colours on one design, and these must be kept clean and clear. If you use the same brush for all the colours, be sure to wash it out carefully after each, drying it with a rag or blotting-paper so that the paint does not become too watery.

16. When the paint is almost dry, lift off the stencil. Take care to lift it off straight upwards—do not slide it about, as this could smudge the pattern where the paint is still wet.

17. Allow the pattern to dry completely—then afterwards you can trim the edges of the card in the normal way—with a steel-edged ruler and the trimming-knife.

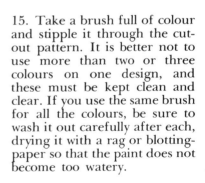

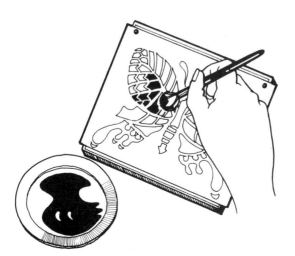

Hints

Trimming-knives or scalpels are very sharp. Do the cutting out slowly and carefully, and make sure you do it in a very good light.

The base card may be white or coloured; or a white or coloured paper stuck onto the base card may also be used. Stencilled patterns take best on a slightly absorbent surface, rather than on a shiny hard one, which is often difficult to print on because the paint lies on the surface and tends to slide and blot.

If you do make a mistake, and paint gets under the parchment to form a small blob, it is possible to retouch the mistake. This should be effective, but avoid doing it too many times on one card as it will look messy and untidy. You are bound to have a number of mistakes at first, so don't get depressed or dispirited.

Instead of putting paint on with a stencil brush, it is also possible to fill in the pattern with coloured felt-tipped pens or coloured pencils. If you are using paint, and you are making a batch of cards each in a different colour, make sure the paint of one colour has dried fully on the stencil before applying the next.

A choice of butterfly designs.

The colour you choose for the base card is important when you are doing stencils, as the background becomes part of the pattern. Try to choose colours that are complementary and blend together, whether all soft, pastel shades, or very bright, cheerful colours. You may emphasize the shape of the butterfly by cutting it out and folding it slightly down the middle. Butterflies are among the most beautiful of nature's creations and lend themselves to any happy occasion. *In colour on page 18.*

22

Storks for the birth of a baby, or perhaps a first birthday. The finished card in the photograph is printed on a pretty, mottled blue-and-pink paper—and so you can make the card before the child is born! On page 78 is an example of a similar design produced in a different way. *In colour on page 18.*

A peony for an invitation. We have shown a finished card in quite restrained colours, to give a classic, formal effect. You may like to use much brighter colours, to produce a quite different impression. This design is particularly suited to conversion into a scraper-board card—you can use the same basic outline, and fill in the veins on the leaves and the stripes on the petals. *In colour on page 23.*

A simple dragon design, specially effective in luminescent colours. Because of its simplicity you can use it for batches of cards, such as invitations. In the photograph you can see not only a finished card made from this design, but also the stencil we used, made from parchment paper. *In colour on page 23.*

For the Jewish New Year, a Hanukkah lamp or menorah. You may like to personalize your cards by printing each one on a different-coloured paper, one for each of your relatives and friends. We show two in the photograph. You can also add glitter as a final touch, to give sparkle and realism to the flames. *In colour on page 23.*

25

Collage

A collage is a picture or design made up from cut-out pieces of paper from different sources (newspapers, magazines, comics, wallpaper, wrapping-paper and so on) or other materials, including fabrics; these are glued onto a base. This kind of assemblage of cut-out pieces makes a wonderful variety or images of decorative patterns. Various other things are sometimes added, such as sand, glitter, sawdust, feathers, sequins, or almost anything else, to produce an interesting, even surprising surface quality. The juxtaposition of printed, painted and added decorative material gives the medium richly inventive qualities, and it has sometimes been incorporated into drawings and paintings by famous artists—Ernst, Schwitters, Braque, Picasso and Matisse have all used the technique of cut, adhesive paper to make pictures.

Materials

Base card
White, coloured or textured card or paper for the background to the collage
Rubber-based gum
Transparent, quick-drying glue
Adhesive tape or drawing-pins (thumb-tacks)
Drawing-board
Collage materials—textured, printed, wrapping, or metallic paper, wallpaper, printed fabrics, glitter, sand, etc.
Scissors, trimming-knife or scalpel
HB pencil
Eraser

What to do

1. Choose the paper, coloured or textured, that is to form the background to the collage, and gum it onto the base card.

2. Tape or pin the card to the drawing-board.

3. Using scissors, trimming-knife or scalpel, cut out from the assembled papers and fabrics the shapes you are going to stick onto the card—if you wish you may lightly draw the shapes out with an HB pencil, and cut along the lines.

4. Put the cut-outs and any other materials you are using in position on the card, and when you have a design you like, glue them in place.

5. Remove any surplus glue with your finger or a piece of clean cloth. Any visible pencil marks can be removed with an eraser.

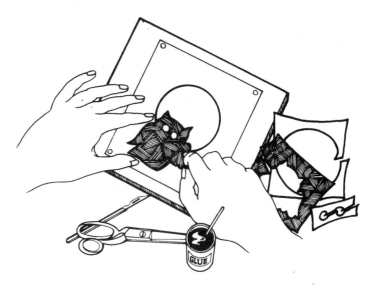

Hints

This technique can be used in a variety of styles—you can incorporate meticulously cut-out illustrations from newspapers, magazines and other graphic sources, or adopt a freer kind of cutting or even tearing out in which the 'accidental' quality of the cutting is actually an important characteristic of the design itself, rather as the line is in a drawing. In effect, you are drawing with scissors. Tearing the paper gives it a furry, rough edge, and a different effect from the sharp cuts of scissors or knife.

Most art stores keep a selection of coloured papers and cards with shiny or matt surfaces. Some specialise in decorative wrapping-papers. On the whole, however, though the colours of these are even, bright and varied, it is often more interesting to keep a selection of cut-out material which you have gathered yourself from odd sources, and which you can incorporate into your designs. It is worth keeping a collection going. You can also buy packets of printed motifs, such as flowers, heads and animals; these were popular in Victorian times and in the 1920s and 1930s, and have since become available again.

For attaching the larger pieces to your collages, the advantage of a rubber-based gum is that the surplus is easily removed and leaves no stain. It may not be strong enough for the smaller pieces, such as sequins, for which a thinner, transparent, quicker-drying glue (not a polystyrene cement) is best. When you use glitter or sand, first apply glue to the area you wish to cover on the card, spread the glitter or sand over it, and then shake off the excess.

For the birthday of a sport-loving friend or relative, or perhaps as a 'good-luck' card before an important match, a pair of tennis racquets. Green is the most suitable background colour here, suggestive of a grass court. You can stick real string onto the racquets, and off-cuts of towelling or leather onto the handle grips. The name of the recipient could be written in where the maker's name normally goes. The racquets themselves are made from cut-out paper. *In colour on page 26.*

A card for a housewarming, or 'welcome home'. It is made with strips of coloured and gummed paper. You could also trace off the design and paint it. *In colour on page 26.*

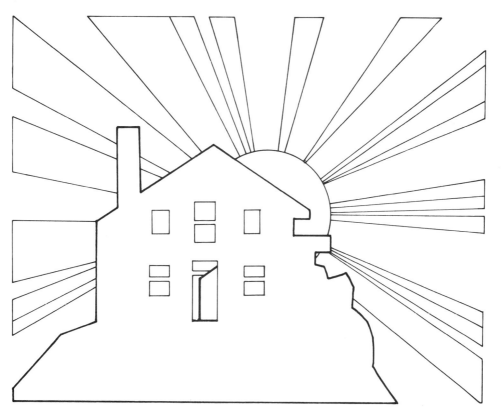

An owl, for Father's Day, or a male birthday. You can make this one either simply with coloured and gummed paper, as we have, or exploit the collage medium further by sticking feathers or large seeds onto the owl. You could also cut out the area of the moon, and stick a piece of silver paper onto the base card where it shows through. *In colour on page 26.*

Another card for a man's birthday. The fish is decorated with sequins. They are threaded onto a length of cotton, glue is applied to the card, and the sequins are firmly pressed down. The fish illustrated in colour is cut from coloured card, but you could also use cloth or tin foil. The waves are glitter, sprinkled onto still-wet glue applied in the shapes required. *In colour on page 26.*

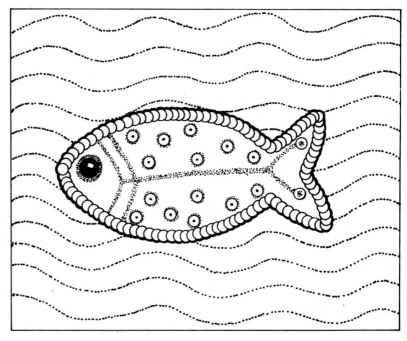

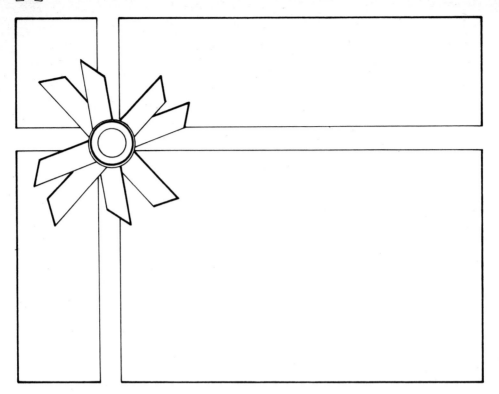

A very quick card to make for a birthday or Christmas. You can use a strip of paper or real ribbon; the bow can be actually tied, or made up from short lengths of paper or ribbon. You can quickly vary the size, shape and colour of the cards if you are making several for your friends. *In colour on page 26.*

A basket of flowers for St Valentine's Day. First you cut out and stick down part of a cake doily, and then cut out the heart from red paper. Pink or red satin would be an alternative. The flowers and basket are the kind of collage motifs which can be bought from art stores and stationery suppliers—you press them out of a sheet and stick them down. *In colour on page 31.*

The black cat is a traditional symbol of good luck. This one is cut from black paper, and sequins are stuck on for decoration. It would be very effective to use a cloth material (velvet would be ideal) for the body and head of the cat, making the whiskers from pipe-cleaners and the eyes from beads or coloured sequins. This design would also work particularly well as a scraper-board card. *In colour on page 31.*

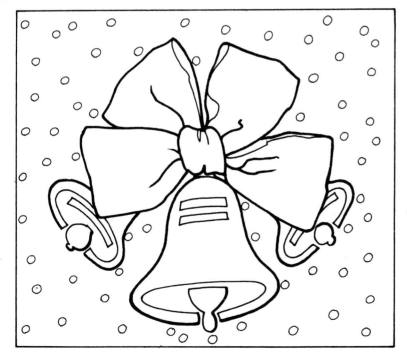

The bow for this New Year or Hogmanay card may be made out of paper or real ribbon or metallic tape. The ribbon has a seasonal tartan pattern and is glued onto bells cut out of silver paper, which in turn are stuck to a coloured base card. *In colour on page 31.*

Just right for a child to make for the birthday of a friend, brother or sister, these two cards are made with heads bought from a stationery store as part of a sheet, pressed out and stuck onto the card. The clothes are made from pieces of paper and sequins, and large sequins are stuck on for the balls in the upper card. *In colour on page 31.*

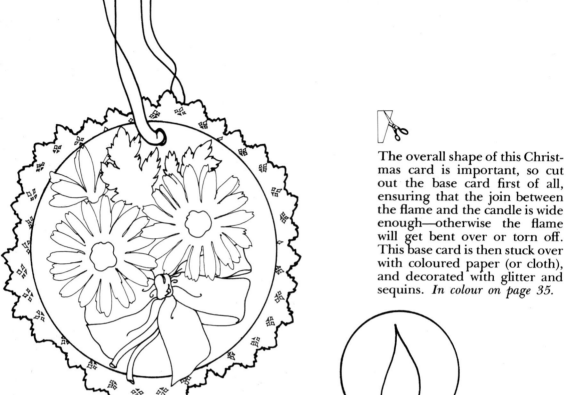

The overall shape of this Christmas card is important, so cut out the base card first of all, ensuring that the join between the flame and the candle is wide enough—otherwise the flame will get bent over or torn off. This base card is then stuck over with coloured paper (or cloth), and decorated with glitter and sequins. *In colour on page 35.*

This hanging card for Mother's Day is very simple to make. The collage materials are stuck onto a disc of green paper, onto the back of which is first glued a cut-out section of a cake doily, showing round the edge as a decorative border. The bow is made from ribbon or strips of paper; the flowers and leaves can be taken from an old hat (you could also use pressed flowers). To make the card sufficiently robust, attach the leaves and the flowers together with cotton or fine wire, and then glue this assembly onto the card. The bow can then be stuck on so as to hide any cotton or wire that is visible. When the design is completely assembled, stick the doily downwards onto a base card, punch a hole in the top edge and thread it with ribbon so that the card scan be hung up. *In colour on page 35.*

This collage is made with natural seeds, and makes a beautiful card for Thanksgiving or Harvest Festival. The base is a hessian material (you could use any material, but choose one with an attractive texture); this is stuck first to a piece of brown paper, which in turn is then stuck to a solid base card. Now you can build up your collage. You will not be able to copy this design exactly—but it does not matter; gather together any natural objects you can find—dried leaves and flowers, fruit from trees, seeds and so on. Spend a little time sorting out the best position for each of the elements in the collage before finally sticking them down. *In colour on page 35.*

This is a card for almost any occasion. Find a small mirror, and stick it firmly onto a base card $\frac{3}{4}''$ (18 mm) larger on all sides. Cover over this card border with $\frac{3}{4}''$-wide ribbon, trimming the ribbon at the corners of the card at 45° to give a mitred effect. You can then write a personal message on the mirror in felt-tip pen, oil pastel or lipstick. *In colour on page 35.*

Potato-cut

Potato-cuts are designs made with potatoes which have had a pattern cut into the flat surface, which is then rubbed in colour; and the pattern is then hand-printed by firmly pressing the potato onto a piece of paper.

This method makes attractive cards; it may also be used for book covers, curtain fabrics, wrapping-paper—we have shown some examples on page 43. It is interesting to see how inventive, rich and varied such an apparently simple technique can be.

Potato-cuts have a characteristic quality, which depends on the texture of the potato itself and how absorbent it is. Even if you repeat the same pattern again and again, it will always seem slightly different because of variations in pressure and moisture. It is this accidental quality which makes potato-cuts so attractive and sympathetic.

Materials

Six potatoes of various sizes
Sharp table-knife or kitchen knife
Trimming-knife or scalpel
White, absorbent paper
Drawing-board
Adhesive tape or drawing-pins (thumb-tacks)
Poster or gouache paints
Water jar
Several small, white paper plates
Blotting-paper

What to do

1. Cut the potatoes in half with the table-knife or kitchen knife.

2. With the scalpel or trimming-knife cut out the desired pattern on the flat, cut surface of the potato to a depth of about a quarter of an inch.

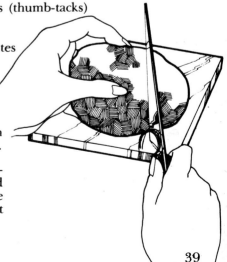

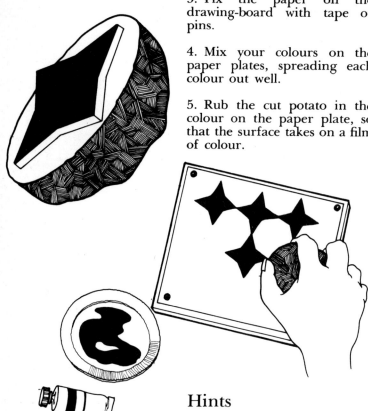

3. Fix the paper on the drawing-board with tape or pins.

4. Mix your colours on the paper plates, spreading each colour out well.

5. Rub the cut potato in the colour on the paper plate, so that the surface takes on a film of colour.

6. Place the potato-cut firmly down on the paper, thus transferring the image onto it from the potato.

7. Repeat the process in different positions on the paper, until you have got the pattern you want. Remember that you can always experiment on a spare piece of paper.

8. If you want to change colours, but continue using the same potato, dip it in water and dry it out on a piece of blotting-paper.

9. Finally, when the paint is dry, the paper can be trimmed and mounted on a piece of card.

Hints

Experiment with the colours, but always make sure you keep the paints fresh and clean. Sometimes you may have to wait for one colour to dry on the paper before you print another one on top—but sometimes you may achieve interesting textures by placing another colour on top of your already printed pattern while it is still wet. This is a matter of experiment.

This blotchy, experimental effect is characteristic of potato-cuts and of hand-printing in general—it can be extremely beautiful. Bold, simple patterns are best; these may be abstract, made from dots, squares, circles, etc., or images, people, animals, flowers, fruit, etc.—all these you can create yourself.

Remember that the image will come out reversed left to right; and in reverse also in the sense that the parts where you have cut will come out white (or whatever colour paper you are using).

Interesting sequences of images can be achieved by progressively cutting away more of the potato between each application to the paper.

With reasonable care you can use the potato for several cards; provided you keep it moist, a potato can even be kept for several hours.

A bouquet for Easter, Mother's Day or a Golden Wedding, built up from several simple potato-cuts. The areas filled in on the diagram are those you cut from the potato. The flowers may be printed in several different colours. *In colour on page 38.*

Another Easter card. Experiment with background papers of different colours to give different effects. The background will amost always be somewhat visible through the printed image. Bear in mind that if you choose a strong background colour it will tend to dull page colours printed on it. *In colour on page 38.*

Another bouquet pattern. These potato-cuts can be most attractive—you could well frame one and hang it on the wall. *In colour on page 38.*

An alternative daisy pattern. Using simple flower motifs it is possible to build up very large, complex designs that can be used over large areas—for wrapping-paper, for example.

Greetings come in many forms. Making your own wrapping-paper gives present-giving a special, personal touch. This motif, simple and yet bold in effect, is very suitable. *In colour on page 43.*

The radial spokes of this motif are all individually printed with a thin wedge of potato—this sort of process can be carried out with any object that will carry the paint satisfactorily. *In colour on page 43.*

A smaller version of the apple motif, for use on a card. Closely spaced, repeated patterns of smaller motifs can give a quite different effect from bold, spacey arrangements. *In colour on page 43.*

We have used this pattern to produce a complete gift set —card, present-tag, and wrapping-paper. *In colour on page 43.*

Below left and right: Simple elements used in different combinations can produce interesting graphic effects for wrapping-paper. *In colour on page 43.*

44

All the designs on this page are alternatives to those illustrated in the photographs. The holly and Christmas Tree designs are traditional in feeling; by contrast we have included a very simple geometric pattern produced entirely by repeated printing with a single triangular potato 'block', and which lends itself to any occasion.

Lino-cut

Many people are familiar with the lino-cut method of producing printed designs—in fact it has been used in the past by many famous artists, such as Picasso and Matisse, to create graphic effects.

Lino-cut is a simple and direct form of printing, and can be used with good results by both adults and children. The principle behind it is that areas about $\frac{3}{4}''$ thick are gouged out of a piece of lino, which is then inked up and printed onto a piece of absorbent paper. The cut-out areas do not collect the ink, and what is actually printed corresponds to what is left of the original surface of the lino.

Lino tends to have a rather crumbly, biscuit-like texture, and so the images it makes are softer than steel engravings, etchings or wood-cuts. On the other hand, it permits a degree of precision and detail that cannot be achieved with potato-cuts, which we looked at earlier. The process is simpler and easier than wood-cuts and the like, and it gives a pleasing decorative effect particularly suitable for greetings cards.

Like stencilling, the lino-cut method is an excellent way of producing not just a single card but also a number, using the same basic design.

Materials

Drawing-board
Tracing-paper
Adhesive tape or drawing-pins (thumb-tacks)
HB pencil
White poster-colour and paint-brush
Carbon paper
H pencil, or ballpoint pen
Trimming-knife or scalpel
Lino-cutting handle and blades
Plastic wood
Sandpaper (fine grade)
Tube of printing-ink (water-based is better): black or dark blue is
    best to start with

Piece of glass about 1' square
Roller (it is quite useful but not essential to have two)
Absorbent paper
Blotting-paper or newspaper
Spoon

What to do

1. Put the pattern to be adapted on your table or drawing-board, facing upwards.

2. Place the tracing-paper over the pattern, and fix it with tape or drawing-pins so that it does not slip while you are tracing.

3. With an HB pencil transfer the pattern onto the tracing-paper in the form of a line drawing.

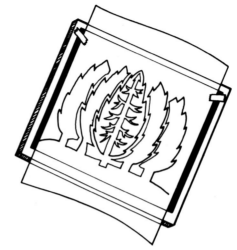

4. If necessary, make the design larger or smaller with the aid of a grid (see page 96).

5. Paint the lino white with poster-colour and allow it to dry.

6. Place the carbon paper face down on the lino and lay the traced drawing on top.

7. Tape or pin lino and design firmly onto the drawing-board so as to avoid movement.

8. With an H pencil or a ball-point pen trace the drawing, so that it is transferred by the carbon paper onto the piece of lino.

9. Remove the carbon paper and the tracing-paper—the design should now be visible on the whitened lino.

10. With the HB pencil shade the areas of the lino to be cut out.

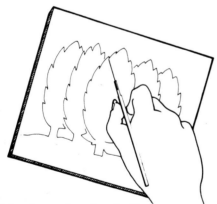

11. With the trimming-knife, scalpel, or flat-bladed attachment of the lino-cutting tool slowly and carefully cut round the edges of the areas to be cut out to a depth of about ¼".

12. Chisel out the shaded areas with the gouging blade of the lino-cutting tool.

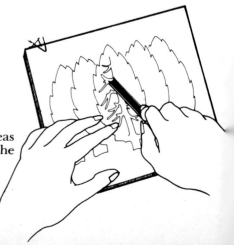

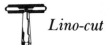

13. If you make mistakes, these may be filled in with plastic wood and smoothed flat with the sandpaper, level with the lino surface, before being cut into again. If you take care, however, you will not make mistakes.

14. Squeeze out some printing-ink onto the piece of glass and roll it out into a thin film with the roller by moving it back and forth several times. Make sure that no fluff or grit gets into the ink.

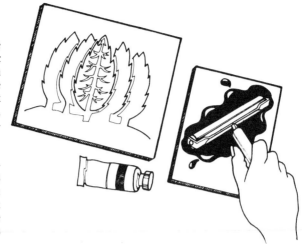

15. With the roller transfer the ink by rolling a thin layer over the lino-cut, so that the uncut surface is entirely covered with a thin layer of ink.

16. Take a piece of paper and lay it carefully on top of the lino-cut. Be careful not to slide it around.

17. Cover the paper with a layer of blotting-paper or newspaper, and with the underneath of the bowl of the spoon rub firmly over the blotting-paper or newspaper backing. Another roller makes things even easier (and of course if you can borrow a special press, this is even better, but not essential).

18. Lift the paper carefully off the lino. You should now have a clear print.

Hints

When you are creating your own designs for lino-cut cards, remember as you first draw them that the areas you cut on the lino will show up as white on a darker ground in the finished card. As with all forms of direct printing, if you want to include letters or numbers, be sure to cut them on the lino reversed left to right. The printed version will be a mirror-image.

If the finished result is too black with smeary edges, you have overloaded the roller when applying the ink; if it is pale and blotchy, you have used too little ink. A little practice is necessary before you can achieve the right density.

You can of course vary the colour of the ink used, depending on the subject matter—you may also vary the colour of the paper you are printing on.

The areas that are shaded in here are the areas to be cut out of the lino. It is possible to print several cards with the lino as first cut, and then clean the lino with water (provided you are using a water-based ink, otherwise you will need turpentine or white spirit). Next cut away the pattern in the lino a little more, and print over the first impressions in a slightly different colour. This process can be continued to produce a very effective result, with a series of superimposed, reducing shapes in different colours. *In colour on page 46.*

A traditional image for Christmas. As with potato-cuts, take care when you choose the colour of the paper you intend to print on. Consider carefully, too, the colours of the inks, which can contrast with, or complement, the background; choose colours which are suitable for the design—green skies and blue Christmas trees would certainly be novel, but may not produce the 'traditional' effect many of us look for in Christmas cards. Remember that for a lino-cut design, where different areas are to be printed in different colours, each colour is printed separately from a separate lino block. You must therefore work out the colour arrangement in advance, and build up the final picture stage by stage. *In colour on page 46.*

Above and top right are two alternative design suggestions for lino-cuts that would be effective simply printed in black ink on white paper, to produce an 'Op Art' effect. They can be used for cards, or for wrapping-paper, identification tags and so on.

Another alternative design that would be ideal for a children's party invitation, using brightly coloured paper or ink.

A design suitable for almost any occasion. Simple but effective, it could be used for other purposes, such as personal stationery.

A lively design with ducks. Lino-cuts are very versatile, and this pattern could be printed onto a broad piece of ribbon to make decorations for Christmas or birthday parties other than cards.

The two animal designs on this page can be used for almost any occasion. Greetings may be sent on a material other than card, and if you use an oil-based ink, designs may be printed on pieces of mirror-glass, or tile, although of course such brittle or fragile materials cannot be sent easily through the mail. Remember that oil-based inks are more difficult than water-based to remove from clothing, and you will need to clean your roller, glass and lino block with turpentine or white spirit.

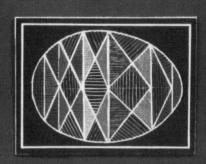

Scraper-board

Scraper-board is a type of card that can be bought in art stores ready coated first with a white, chalky substance and then with a layer of black ink. When you scrape the black surface, the white underneath shows through. The result is a crisp and sparkling black-and-white design.

This medium is used a great deal commercially because its clear-cut graphic quality is particularly suitable for photographic reproduction, and comes out well even when printed on inferior newsprint.

Scraper-board designs may look like etchings in reverse —that is, white on black—and they may be very rich in texture. The method is especially attractive when used for greetings cards, with its highly 'finished' quality, and the cards that you make could well be mounted up and framed by the recipient.

Materials

HB pencil
White paper or tracing-paper
Scraper-board
Base card
Rubber-based gum
Drawing-board
Adhesive tape
Carbon paper or chalk
H pencil or ballpoint pen
Soft, white, chalk pencil
Scraper-board tool with alternative blades

What to do

1. With the HB pencil draw the guiding outline for your design on a piece of white paper, or tracing-paper if you are using one of the designs we have illustrated, or any other existing design.

2. Stick your piece of scraper-board to the base card with the gum before you transfer the design onto it—scraper-board is rather brittle, and this helps to ensure that you will not crack it.

3. Tape the scraper-board and base card firmly to the drawing-board (use tape rather than pins, which make a hole which would be visible afterwards).

4. Cover the scraper-board with a sheet of carbon paper, carbon side down.

5. Lay the paper with the design over the carbon paper, fixing it down to the drawing-board with tape or pins so that it does not slip.

6. With an H pencil or a ball-point pen trace over the design, thus imprinting it through the carbon paper onto the scraper-board.

7. Take away the design and the carbon paper, and hold the scraper-board up to the light at an angle so you can see the pattern on it. You may have to look quite carefully, as the colours are sometimes very similar.

8. Alternatively trace the design onto tracing paper, rub white chalk over the back, and use the chalked tracing instead of the carbon paper in steps 4-7; the marks will show up white. Another method of putting the design outline onto the scraper-board is to draw it out directly onto the board with a soft, white, chalky pencil which may be brushed off afterwards.

9. When you have all the large, guiding patterns marked out on your scraper-board, etch them out with the scraper blade. The spaces can be filled in with scraped designs of various textures.

Hints

As you can see from the illustrations, basic designs can be decorated with a number of different scraper patterns. The possibilities are infinite, and so that you can make the best of them it is a good idea to buy several extra sheets of scraper-board. This way you can play around, discover how to make use of the different blades of the scraper tool, make patterns and get the feel of the medium. You will discover all sorts of interesting effects which you will be able to use in your cards.

If you make a mistake, it is possible to paint it out with black ink, and then redraw on top when the ink is dry. It is also possible to tint the white design with paint or ink. Be careful when you do this—some felt marker-pens contain a solvent which dissolves some of the black on the scraper-board, with muddy and unattractive results. Carry out a test first on a small, spare piece of board.

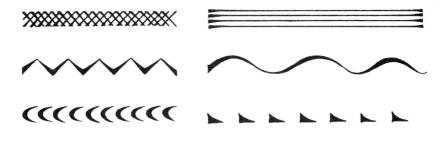

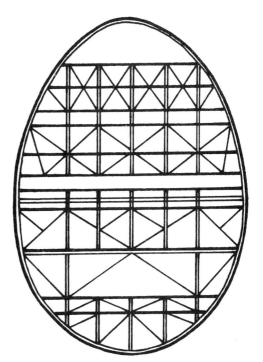

A simple Easter Egg design that you could embellish with the name of the person who is to be given the card. *See page 54.*

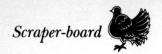

This design, which is suitable for almost any occasion, shows how a fairly formal pattern can be used to gain a very pretty effect, contrasting with the sharply geometric designs on this and the previous page. This effect can be heightened by tinting in some of the white lines with ink or paint. *See page 54.*

Another Easter Egg. A formal, rectangular border surrounding the egg gives the card a 'finished' appearance. Experiment with your cards—you will often find that the imaginative use of borders offers a whole new set of variations on a basic design. *In colour on page 54.*

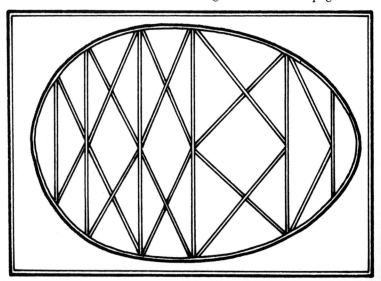

This fish design, suitable for Thanksgiving or similar occasions, looks complex at first sight. But the joy of the scraper-board medium is that you can devote a lot of time and effort to intricate patterns and textures; or you can content yourself with a simpler pattern, and still achieve a dramatic and quite professional result. *See page 54.*

Birds, especially those for the table, are traditionally associated with Christmas, Thanksgiving, or Easter. Perhaps you could give your celebrations a consistent artistic theme, not only by sending your own cards with this pattern, but also by reducing the design in size, and using it for place settings at the dining-table, with the name of each guest written in below. *See page 54.*

21
Today

Some finished cards using the
tracing and colouring method.

Tracing and colouring

Traced cards are simply cards consisting of a line-drawn design which can then be coloured or decorated as you wish. As a basis for your line design you can either use one of the patterns illustrated here, or indeed almost any of the cards in the book. If you wish, you can incorporate design ideas from other sources—you could take flower patterns, for example, from photographs, or decorative wrapping paper or wallpaper. Almost any illustrative material is a potential basis for a traced and coloured card.

Materials

Drawing-board
Tracing-paper
Adhesive tape or drawing-pins (thumb-tacks)
HB pencils
Water-colour paper
Carbon paper
H pencil or ballpoint pen
Paint brushes
Water jar
Blotting-paper, rag, or paper tissue
Designers' colour
Paper plates for mixing colours
Felt-tipped pens or crayons

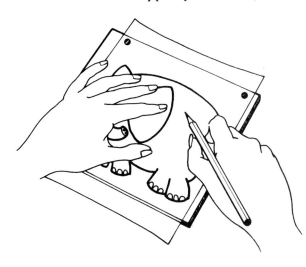

What to do

1. Place the original for your design on the drawing-board.

2. Lay the tracing-paper over the top, and fix it down with adhesive tape or drawing-pins so that it does not slip.

3. With an HB pencil trace off your basic design.

4. We recommend you to enlarge the design if necessary (see on page 96).

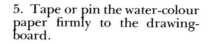

5. Tape or pin the water-colour paper firmly to the drawing-board.

6. Cover it with a sheet of carbon paper, carbon side down.

7. Put the traced design on top, fixing this down in turn.

8. With an H pencil or a ball-point pen trace over the design again, imprinting it through the carbon paper onto the water-colour paper. Remove the tracing-paper and carbon.

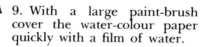

9. With a large paint-brush cover the water-colour paper quickly with a film of water.

10. Blot the paper with blotting-paper, a rag or paper tissue, leaving the paper faintly damp.

11. Now paint in the colours.

12. As an alternative to steps 9-11, felt-tipped pens or crayons can be used.

Hints

The design that you trace from the original pattern is best kept fairly simple and used simply as a guide for the colouring stage. This will permit a freer use of colour than too much fiddly detail at the beginning.

Make sure that the colours are clean and clear. Do not put them on heavily or densely. You can always add another wash of colour, but once a wash has been put on you cannot easily remove it. If you are quick, minor mistakes can sometimes be removed with blotting-paper.

If you add details of one colour over another colour, give the first layer of paint time to dry almost completely. Otherwise the effect will be unpleasant and muddy.

Designers' colour looks best when applied thinly, so that you can see the paper underneath. The white of the paper reflects the light and gives the painted design a particular translucent brilliance. Water-colour paints can give even better results, but these need to be handled with considerable expertise—for most of us designers' colour is the better choice.

Just right for children's birthdays or party invitations, this simple elephant design can be coloured in by the youngest. *See page 60.*

A border design, which you can use to frame a photograph or drawing; or you could write an invitation or any other personal greeting in the middle. *See page 60.*

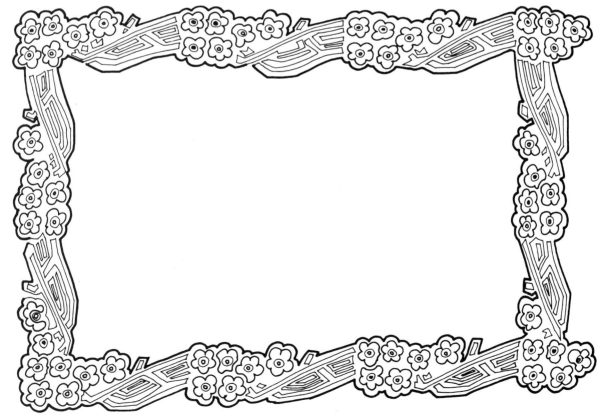

Tracing and colouring is one of the methods best suited for one-off cards; but it is quite possible to produce batches of cards using for example the invitation design shown here. The design is first drawn clearly and neatly in black, and then photocopied. Cut out the photocopies and paste them neatly onto base cards. If you would like to add a personal touch to each invitation, colour it separately by hand. *See page 60.*

This design could be used in conjunction with the collage method, decorated with real seeds, straw and feathers. Note how the circular border ties the whole pattern together. *See page 60.*

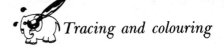

Another treatment of the bird motif, in an attractive round shape. The shapes to which you cut out your cards can offer almost as much scope for the imagination as the use of different subjects. *In colour on page 66.*

Bells and holly for Christmas. To make the design suitable for a wedding, do not include the holly, and vary the colours. Simple, traditional designs can very often be adapted for a number of different occasions in this way. *In colour on page 66.*

For this one we have used a combination of paper cut-outs and tracing. The garlands and flowers consist of coloured, gummed paper, onto which the pattern is carefully traced and painted. The design would look very effective as a collage, with crumpled tissue paper, dried flowers and real ribbon. *In colour opposite.*

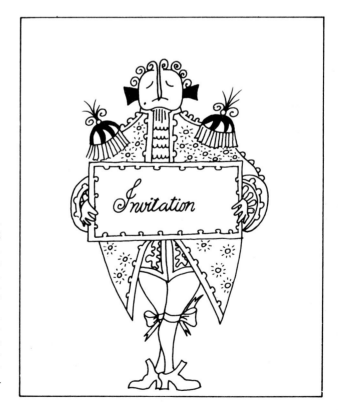

Here is another design for an invitation. We have presented it in the photograph opposite as a traced and coloured card. As with the design on page 64, a batch of invitations can be made by tracing (and enlarging if necessary) the basic design in black, photocopying it, and colouring, trimming and mounting the copies. Alternatively, the design could be adapted for the lino-cut method. *In colour opposite.*

 Another design for a 'flower painting'. This design, reminiscent of tapestry motifs, is nostalgic of high summer, and may be used for any happy occasion. *In colour on page 66.*

An unusual card for Christmas—you can open the 'door', and through it look into a warm and inviting room with seasonal decorations. Remember to trace and colour the door on both sides. It can then be hinged to the rest of the card with a strip of transparent adhesive tape; or you can cut it out with two tags on the hinge edge, one near the top and the other near the bottom, and then cut two vertical slots in the main part of the card, through which the tags can be fitted and stuck to the back. If the whole design is then mounted on a stiffer base card, the door 'hinges' at the back will be invisible. You can adapt the design so that the door or the room inside is like your own; or you can change the picture inside to make the card into a house-warming or birthday greeting. Try to think of other ways in which a three-dimensional effect can be used. *In colour on page 66.*

A cherry tree, and a card for any occasion. The design can be traced and painted, cut out, and glued onto a base card of a contrasting colour. It is particularly effective as we have shown it in the photograph—here, silver designers' gouache has been used for the background of the design itself. *In colour opposite.*

An easy way to enlarge this Father Christmas (see page 96) is to trace it, make a grid over it at the present size, and then redraw it straight onto graph paper. As both the design and the background can be coloured in, none of the graph lines will show. *In colour opposite.*

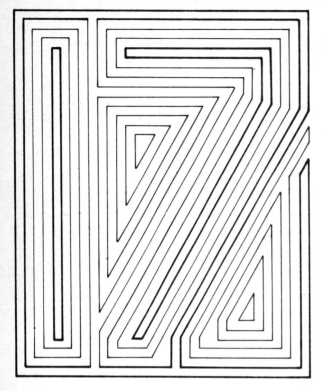

Two easy-to-do birthday cards for teenagers. They can be drawn and painted straight onto graph paper, and so it is very easy to get the lines straight and parallel. Experiment first on a spare piece of graph paper—the small squares give you great possibilities for variation. *In colour on page 71.*

Another birthday card, simple and effective. Round cards need a very simple support to make them stand up (see page 101). Any number can be put in the centre, and the colours varied to suit your taste. *In colour on page 71.*

Two versions of a really novel card for any kind of 'thank-you'. The peppermill design in a border is traced onto a coloured envelope, real pepper-corns are slipped inside, and you have a token of gratitude to send to a friend after a dinner-party, for example You can develop the idea, using flower seeds you have collected from your own garden, and drawing a corresponding flower on the front of the envelope. *In colour on page 71.*

Traditional symbols can be very effective. Doves represent peace and harmony, and this is a good design to give to a relative or friend on his or her engagement. Note how the cutting of the outer edge is used as part of the design. *In colour on page 71.*

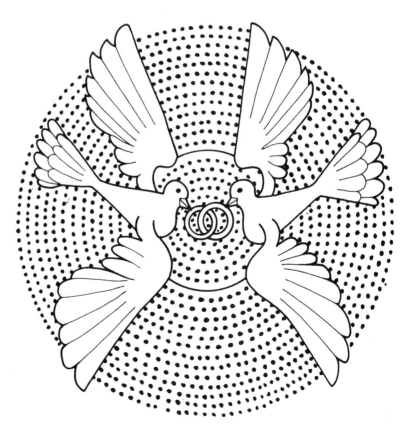

Blots

The Chinese and Japanese used ink blots as an art form in themselves. The final shape of a blot is largely a matter of chance, and this is the charm of the medium—they noticed that these accidents often suggested phenomena such as landscapes, animals, faces and other natural forms.

The initial blot might also be a basis for decoration and development of some astonishingly beautiful images. We think that you, too, might find this 'accidental' method an excellent starting-off point in inventing fresh ideas, and developing your own creative powers and imagination.

Materials

Absorbent paper
Brushes
Coloured inks
Blotting-paper
Base card or paper
Rubber-based gum

What to do

1. Place the absorbent paper on a flat surface.

2. Dip a brush into some ink, diluted if necessary with water, and drop a blob onto the paper.

3. Fold the paper into two and press together.

4. Open out the paper.

5. Blot it if you wish, or allow it to dry if you have produced a dynamic pattern.

6. Add other blots of ink of the same or different colours.

7. You may continue the process, building up several layers until you have something which pleases you.

8. Mount the paper on the base cardboard.

Hints

This is a 'once-only' process—the pattern is unique and cannot be repeated exactly for a number of cards. However, there is no reason why you should not produce a number of individual cards reasonably easy and quickly. You will need some space on a table to let them dry, and while the first blot of ink on one card is drying you may be adding to another.

It is most important, however, that each design is carefully mounted on its base card rather like a jewel or a precious piece of fabric. The design is the result of a carefully controlled accident and should be no less highly regarded than a consciously tight and graphic one.

The blot method produces symmetrical and yet unpredictable shapes. If combined with other methods such as collage, blots can be made into exotic and colourful images.

Here, blots are combined with drawn lines and shapes to produce a pair of lively performing animals.

Cut-out

These are cards made with a sheet of paper from which a pattern is cut out rather as one cuts out a stencil. The cut-out pattern is then mounted on a card of a contrasting colour, which shows through the 'windows'. The Mexicans employ this method in their traditional folk art in a form known as 'papal piccato', which they use for making flags or small private altar coverings.

Because they take some time to make, cut-out cards are recommended for special occasions, such as christenings, weddings, etc.; afterwards they may be kept and even framed as a memento of the occasion.

Materials

Drawing-board
Tracing-paper
Adhesive tape or drawing-pins (thumb-tacks)
HB pencil
Coloured or metallic paper
Carbon paper or chalk
H pencil or ballpoint pen
Trimming-knife or scalpel
Rubber-based gum or quick-drying glue
Base card

What to do

1. Put the pattern to be used—either one in the book or one that you have found yourself—on the drawing-board.

2. Put a sheet of tracing-paper over the top and fix it with adhesive tape or drawing-pins so that it does not slip.

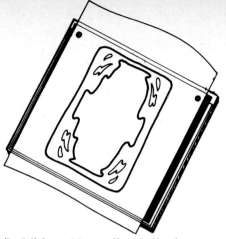

3. With an HB pencil trace the pattern onto the tracing-paper. If you are adapting a pattern, keep the tracing fairly simple.

4. We suggest you enlarge the pattern if necessary by using a grid (see page 96).

5. Tape or pin your coloured or metallic paper to the drawing-board.

6. Lay a sheet of carbon paper on top, and then the tracing-paper, fixing it in position with either tape or pins.If you are using black card, chalk the back of the tracing paper instead of using carbon paper.

7. With an H pencil or ballpoint pen trace over the design, imprinting it through the carbon paper onto the coloured or metallic paper.

8. Take the coloured paper and shade the areas to be cut away. As when cutting out a stencil, remember to leave 'bridges' where necessary, so that pieces of the pattern do not fall out where you have cut all the way round.

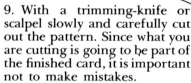

9. With a trimming-knife or scalpel slowly and carefully cut out the pattern. Since what you are cutting is going to be part of the finished card, it is important not to make mistakes.

10. Lightly glue the cut-out paper and place it carefully onto the base card.

Hints

In order for the pattern to be as effective as possible, the base card, or paper, and the cut-out paper pattern should be of two strongly contrasting colours and tones.

There are ways in which this basic method may be varied. For example, before the cut pattern is stuck to the base card some of the 'window' may be covered over with small pieces of different-coloured paper stuck on from the back. Or the base card can be covered with a sheet of clear or coloured acetate or cellophane before the pattern is stuck on. If the clear cellophane appearing through the holes is coloured with a felt pen, the effect is rather like a stained-glass window.

Cut-out

A card for the birth of a baby. The main part of the design is cut from a sheet of coloured paper, which is then stuck to a base card. The attractive, frilly border is made by folding a sheet of paper into halves, then quarters and then eighths; holes are then cut right through, and the sheet of paper opened out again. You could also cut the border from a paper cake doily. *In colour on page 78.*

Another card for a baby's birth which, with very little adaptation, could also serve as a Christmas card. The pattern is cut from cardboard covered with shiny metal foil. With a complex pattern it is well worth tracing the design onto the sheet of card or paper and shading in the areas to be cut. This way a much more planned and 'professional' effect will be achieved. *In colour on page 78.*

A 'stained-glass-window' card for Christmas—you can use the same method for any religious festival. To make the one illustrated take a sheet of base card, crease it and fold it down the middle. Cut the top into a curve by cutting through both the 'front' and the 'back' simultaneously—this way the final curve will be symmetrical. Open it out, and lay it down flat. Stick a sheet of black paper over the front. Trace the design, enlarged if necessary, onto the black paper, using white chalk on the back of the tracing paper, so that you can see the lines afterwards. Shade in the areas to be cut out, and then cut them. Now you put in your 'stained glass'. Experiment with coloured acetate or tissue paper to see which colour looks best where, cut it into pieces the right size and stick over the back of the 'windows'. A quicker but less neat method is to cover the whole of the back of the card with a sheet of clear acetate, and then colour in the windows with paint, felt-tip pen, or ink. *In colour on page 78.*

Cut out the basic butterfly shape, including the open areas in the wings. The finished card photographed was made by sticking pieces of coloured paper on the back of the butterfly cut-out so that they show through the holes. Try out several combinations of colours until you have an arrangement you like, then stick them in position. Then mount the completed butterfly onto a base card. *In colour on page 78.*

Here is a frame in which you can mount a photograph of yourself or one of the family, perhaps to send to a distant relative at Christmas. The photograph is placed behind the frame, and the whole assembly is then stuck down to a base card. Rather than having a photo printed specially to the size and shape of the frame, design the frame to fit the photo. You could also use the frame to decorate an invitation. *In colour on page 78.*

This card and the one on the opposite page are simple to make but attractive when complete. Trace the design, enlarged or reduced as necessary, onto a sheet of black card. Instead of carbon paper, you could use white chalk rubbed onto the back of tracing-paper—this will show up on the black card. Shade and cut out the design, and then place pieces of coloured paper behind it. Experiment with different colours and placings before you finally stick the colours in position. An alternative method is to stick a strip of white paper behind the black cut-out and then colour in the white areas from the front with paint, crayons, or felt-tipped pens. The front of the cards can be decorated with strips of coloured paper or other materials. *In colour on page 83.*

Folding and Cutting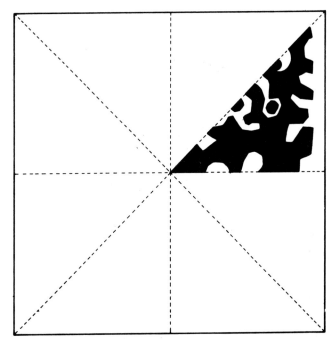

Here we see how two of the cards illustrated in colour on page 83 were made. That on the left was made from a sheet of coloured paper; it was folded into quarters and then pieces were torn out. The one on the right was folded into eighths before being cut with scissors. You can go on folding indefinitely, but too many folds can make the paper too thick to cut or tear. The resulting pattern can be stuck onto a background paper of a contrasting colour, and then, to vary the effect, you can stick small, torn or cut shapes into the larger holes.

Cards made in this way are a variation on the theme of cut-paper cards already described. They, too, achieve their effect by the use of one or more paper patterns glued onto a background of a contrasting colour. The difference is that by folding the paper before you cut out the pattern, you can achieve a design that is exactly symmetrical when the paper is opened out. If you fold the paper more than once, and then cut the pattern, you will achieve a symmetrical pattern of even greater complexity.

You can add variety to the design by building up the pattern on your card out of several folded pieces of paper of different colours, cutting them, opening them out and mounting them individually.

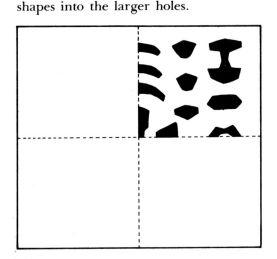

If you want your finished pattern to be representational rather than abstract, you will find that it is quite difficult to cut a folded piece of paper and predict exactly what it is going to look like when opened out. The solution is to draw a rough pattern of the finished design on a spare piece of paper first, and work out the colour scheme. Then you can produce each symmetrical element in the pattern in turn, drawing a line down the middle of it and tracing half of the motif onto one side of your folded, coloured paper, then cutting it out, unfolding it and sticking the completed, cut-out motif onto the background.

You can develop your own ideas from traditional designs, such as this Father Christmas. He could be shown as a full-length figure, with sequins for his eyes, and real buttons on his jacket. *In colour on page 86.*

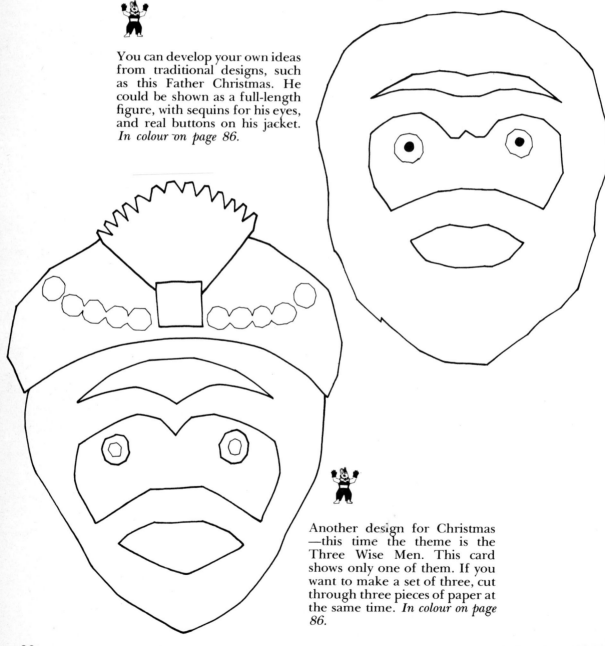

Another design for Christmas —this time the theme is the Three Wise Men. This card shows only one of them. If you want to make a set of three, cut through three pieces of paper at the same time. *In colour on page 86.*

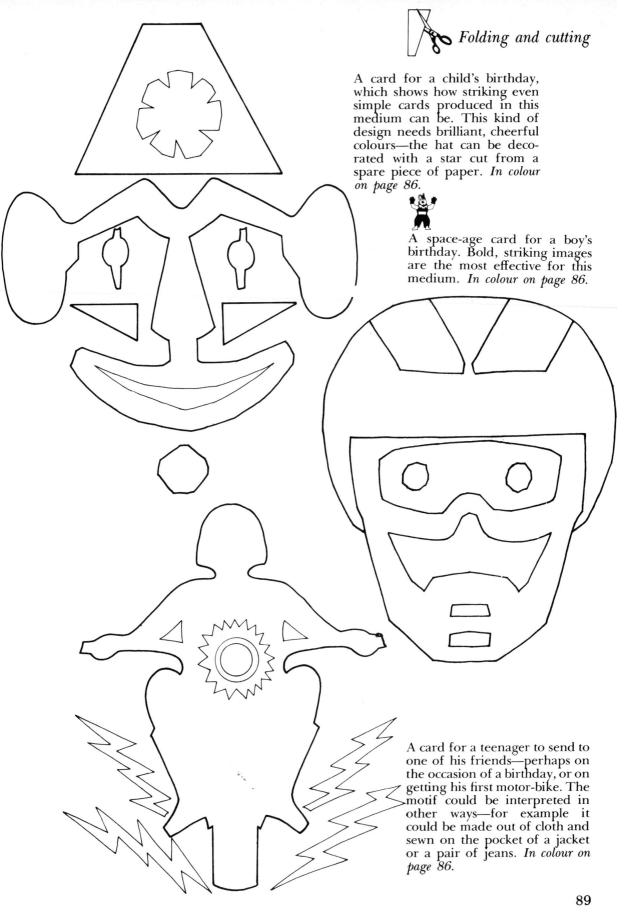

A card for a child's birthday, which shows how striking even simple cards produced in this medium can be. This kind of design needs brilliant, cheerful colours—the hat can be decorated with a star cut from a spare piece of paper. *In colour on page 86.*

A space-age card for a boy's birthday. Bold, striking images are the most effective for this medium. *In colour on page 86.*

A card for a teenager to send to one of his friends—perhaps on the occasion of a birthday, or on getting his first motor-bike. The motif could be interpreted in other ways—for example it could be made out of cloth and sewn on the pocket of a jacket or a pair of jeans. *In colour on page 86.*

Silhouette

Silhouette cards are produced in the same way as cut-paper cards, and the step-by-step instructions on pages 79-80 can be followed for silhouettes too.

What makes silhouettes special is not so much the method as the graphic effect to which it is put. Silhouette images are strong, dramatic images, consisting usually of two basic, contrasting colours. They are generally representational rather than abstract, and consist of the outline only of the subject you are depicting.

The traditional silhouette (named after an 18th-century French politician whose tough economic policies are thought to have made this cheap and simple form of art popular) is a black design on a white background. In the 18th and 19th centuries it became a very widespread art form, especially used for portraiture. If you visit an old house furnished in period style, you are quite likely to find on the walls small, silhouette head-portraits, perhaps of members of the owner's family. These portraits are very delicate and precise, and in time an elaborate filigree style was developed, especially popular in the 1920s. One of the most distinguished artists using the medium was Lotte Reineger, who made a full-length cartoon film entirely in silhouette, as well as illustrating a number of books.

For making greetings cards, perhaps it is most effective to steer clear of elaborate, delicate and fragile fretwork cutting —concentrate on simple, bold images; we feel that the classic black-on-white colour combination is still the most rewarding, but a limited use of additional colour, such as in some of the cards illustrated on page 90, can give a good effect.

It is quite easy to produce a traced outline, as a basis for your design, which is a good likeness of a friend or a relative. Tape a large sheet of tracing-paper onto a vertical sheet of glass or a window. On the other side place the sitter, and behind him or her a strong lamp, preferably one with a small, concentrated light source. This should throw a sharp shadow of the sitter's profile onto the glass, and you can trace it on the paper on the other side of the glass. It is fascinating how often just an outline of someone's profile can be instantly recognisable.

A card for a wedding or any anniversary. *In colour opposite.*

When someone you know retires from work, you can send him or her your good wishes with this peaceful country scene. Again, the card may be made in the traditional black and white, or a more definite mood created by the choice of a restful colour for the back-ground. *In colour on page 90.*

This is a card to wish someone 'Bon voyage', or 'Happy vacation'. Boats suggest to us move-ment and excitement—compare the angular treatment of this design with the more restful shapes in the card above. *In colour on page 90.*

Father's Day would be a suitable occasion for this design, as would any time you want to say 'Congratulations' for a special achievement. *In colour on page 90.*

This Hallowe'en card shows what can be achieved when the medium used and the subject-matter are well suited to one another. The stark contrasts of the silhouette here produce a dark and sinister atmosphere! *In colour on page 90.*

A fairytale castle makes a wonderful symbol for an engagement, wedding, or anniversary. Silhouettes are often most effective in the traditional black and white, but a careful additional use of colour, as in the finished card we have illustrated, can give a special, romantic effect. *In colour on page 90.*

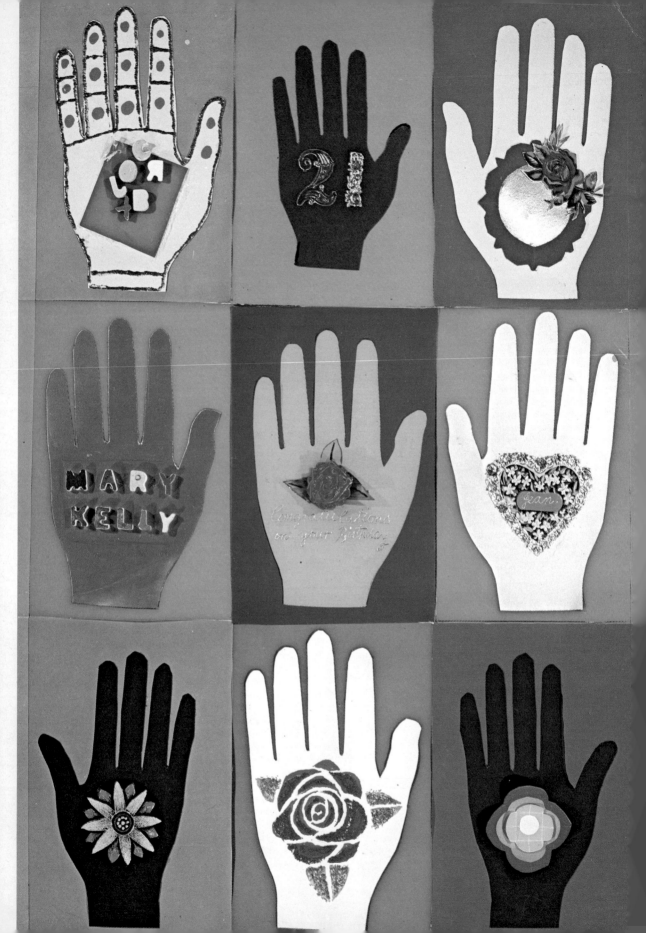

Mixed media

Interesting and surprising designs may be created by combining a number of techniques in one card. For instance, you could take a cut-out pattern of coloured papers (which you have bought) and add to this a paper collage on which you have printed a potato—or lino-cut, or stencilled some pattern or device of your own. Opposite we show different ways of treating a simple hand shape.

You could also use one of your lino-cuts in black-and-white and (as in the Christmas Tree card on page 50) add silver dust to make it glitter with frost; or you could add cut-out collage figures such as the red-coated Santa Claus. In this way one basic design can be adapted for different uses, or made suitable for either adults or children.

Another starting-off point is to make a series of blot-patterned cards and then incorporate cut-out paper shapes, printed cut-outs from magazines and so on, which you may have collected over a period of time. Thus the shape of the blot may be turned into any picture that it suggests to you. The fun and interest of this sort of procedure is that until you yourself have made the initial 'accidental' marks you will not know what to do beforehand; it is the marks themselves which will stimulate your powers of inventiveness and imagination. These marks may suggest landscapes, faces, trees, and so on, which you may elaborately build up. There is no need for them to be representational every time—they do not always have to be a picture of something specific; they may develop into beautiful, abstract design patterns such as you find on carpets and fabrics.

By combining different media in this way it is possible to make joke cards which would amuse a relative or friend. The use of collage material, combined with other effects (as in a collage by Max Ernst), may have a magical or surrealist effect, such as a fairy story.

From now on you are entirely on your own. We wish you much enjoyment and creative pleasure.

Enlarging a design

Many of the designs in this book can be reproduced at the size they are printed; you can trace them off the page directly. On the other hand, you may wish to make them bigger (or smaller). Trace the design onto a sheet of tracing paper, then pin the tracing over a sheet of graph paper. Draw a grid pattern over the design using the graph lines $\frac{1}{2}''$ apart (or it may be 1 cm) as a guide. A useful short cut is to trace the design onto tracing paper already printed with a grid, like graph paper. On another sheet of paper draw another grid increased in size by the amount you want to enlarge the design. Number the lines in both grids to avoid mistakes, and then draw the enlarged design in the corresponding squares on the larger grid.

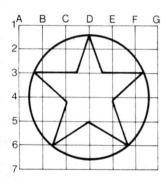

Above: This is how your original design will look after you have traced it and drawn a grid over it. On the right, a grid has been drawn twice the size, and the design drawn onto it, following the squares as a guide.

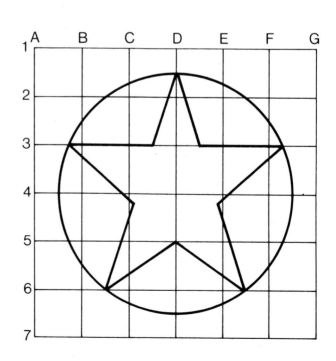

Converting a design

The designs in this book have been illustrated in chapters dealing each with a particular technique. However, it is often possible to produce broadly the same design with a number of techniques—the choice is yours. The effect will be slightly different in each case, according to the method you choose, and to illustrate how a very basic motif can make quite a range of impressions, we are showing you a series of different interpretations on this page. When converting a design from one medium to another, try to exploit the particular qualities of each one.

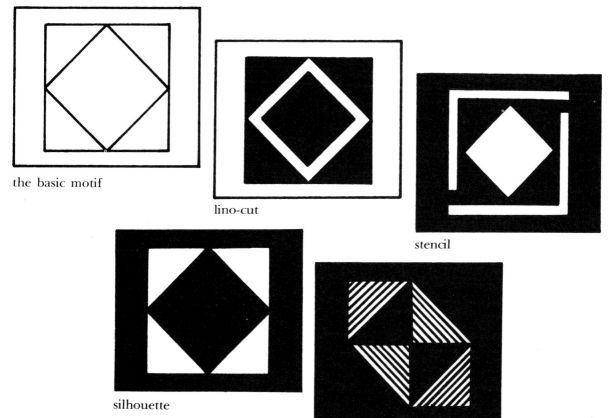

the basic motif

lino-cut

stencil

silhouette

scraper-board

Ideas for lettering

If you would like to use lettering in order to make your card more formal and finished, or as a design idea in itself, you can use some form of 'printing'—though naturally you should use your own signature. In general, if you simply draw out lettering by hand, it is very difficult to get any sort of 'finished' quality. Sometimes it is even better not to try, and simply to write the whole message in your own handwriting.

However, there are other methods which, if carefully used, can produce a very good result. We will describe four of them.

Dry-transfer lettering

This lettering is bought from art stores and stationers in the form of sheets of letters. You can buy different sizes, different type-faces, and even nowadays different colours, besides black and white. Nowadays most commercial studios which need finished lettering use the dry-transfer method. when a quick, professional effect is required.

It is a good idea to obtain a catalogue of type-styles which are produced by the manufacturers before you begin. As the range of styles is so large, you will be sure to find something suitable for your purposes. Furthermore, some of the type-faces may give you a few new ideas, and you can design your lettering with a particular style in mind, which is a help.

It is essential to plan out your lettering in rough first. Take a piece of white paper the same size as the part of the card where the lettering is to appear, and rule horizontal lines across it on which to sketch out your lettering design in pencil. You can also use lined paper. The important thing is to design the lettering so it will fit properly into the card area—you do not want your lettering crushed up against the edge, or running off the page. Work out your layout with reference to the size and style of the lettering you have chosen in the catalogue. All this is worth spending a little time over—you will probably need an eraser until you have the pattern of letters you like. Be patient.

When you are happy with this, lightly draw the horizontal guide line from your sketch onto the card itself. The rest of the process is simple, provided you follow the instructions on the dry-transfer lettering sheet. Find the first letter you need on the sheet of type you have chosen. Place the sheet carefully face downwards so that the base of the letter just touches the horizontal guide line, and so that the letter is upright. With a small, smooth-pointed tool such as a knitting needle or ballpoint pen, press down on the lettering, moving the point all over the back of the letter, transferring it onto the card. Make sure all the letter comes off the backing-sheet. Keeping an eye on the spacing of the letters, as well as their order, in your sketch, proceed with this method until you have transferred all the letters. If you damage any, print over them with a fresh letter. If you make a mistake, a razor blade or your scalpel or trimming-knife will lift off the transferred letter. Finally, place a clean piece of paper over the lettering, and with a teaspoon rub over your letter design to ensure that all the letters are firmly stuck down; then take a soft eraser or putty rubber kneaded to a point, and rub away the pencil guide lines. Your lettering is now complete. You may spray the lettering with a spray fixative which art stores sell for the purpose—this helps prevent damage and peeling.

Stencil lettering

There are two forms of stencil lettering which can be bought at stores which sell supplies for artists and draughtsmen. One is a bold but stylistically rather limited range of lettering cut from parchment paper, the letters ranging in height from one to three inches. The other is cut from clear acetate plastic, and comes in the form of a rule. This is used by draughtsmen and architects in drawing plans. In this case the letters are smaller, from half an inch to an inch high.

For this method, too, plan out your lettering in rough, using horizontally ruled lines on another piece of paper. Then lightly pencil the lines in on your card. With the card firmly pinned or taped to the drawing-board stencil the letters one by one, checking the spacing with your rough sketch. The parchment-paper stencils may be done in the same way as the designs for stencilled cards (see page 19), using a brushful of colour, a coloured pencil or a felt pen. For the plastic-rule letters you will need a pencil or a fine fibre pen. Architectural draughtsmen use a specially made pen with a nib head which slots into the letter track. These tend to be expensive, particularly for once-only use, but for a number of cards it is an easy, convenient and efficient way to do this method properly, and could well be worth the cost. Besides, you can use it for other purposes—labels for baggage, files, cans, spice-bottles, etc. You will need a special ink that does not coagulate.

When you have stencilled all the lettering, and any paint is completely dry, erase any guide lines. The lettering is now ready.

Cut-out lettering

This is really a form of collage (see page 27). Letters, whole words, or even whole messages can be cut from magazines and newspapers (and even old cards!).

Lightly pencil in a horizontal guide line on your card. Having cut out your letters and words, arrange them carefully along the line. If the letters are of different heights and dimensions, or even of different colours, make use of this in an amusing decorative scheme, an integral part of the overall design of the card. The lettering can perhaps be put against a background of a different colour—the possibilities are endless. It is worth building up a collection of letters and words for just this purpose. Sometimes the particularly interesting ones will suggest overall card designs to you.

When the letters have been arranged in the order and position you want, carefully stick them down with a rubber-based gum. When it is dry, rub away any surplus, and erase any visible guidelines.

Trimming, mounting, hingeing and stands

The way you finish your cards is almost as important as the design you put on them, if you are aiming at an attractive and 'professional' result. Here we show some of the basic points. Many of the designs will look best if trimmed and mounted onto a base—perhaps folded so that a personal message can appear on the base card opposite the design.

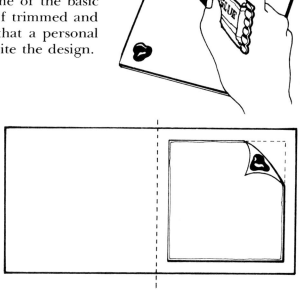

Top, and right: After trimming your design neatly with a steel-edged rule and trimming knife or scalpel, mount it neatly on a base card, using glue sparingly (say, at the four corners only, as shown here). A rubber-based gum is best, because you can easily rub off any excess.

Below: If you want to fold a card so it stands up, draw a faint pencil dotted line along the fold, and then score the line lightly with a scalpel or trimming knife and your steel-edged rule. The card should then fold neatly.

Below, centre and right: Even flat or irregularly shaped cards can be made to stand up if you glue onto the back a simple cardboard prop.

Making your own envelopes

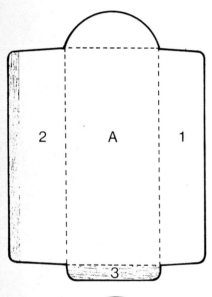

At the beginning of the book we gave you a number of dimensions of envelopes which are commercially available either in the United Kingdom, the United States, or both. However, not all stores will stock the size you want, and it is better not to be restricted by the standard shapes when you are making your cards. In fact, you can easily make your own envelopes, using the diagrams below as a guide for two basic envelope shapes.

The envelope will be cut out from a flat sheet of paper. Pencil out the cutting and folding lines on the paper before you start. The dotted lines in the diagrams indicate the outside edges of the final envelope, so these should make a rectangle (A) slightly larger than your card, which will then slip in easily. Cut out the outside edge (shown by the solid lines). Half fold in the flaps, using the edge of a steel rule to help you get straight folds. Apply glue to the shaded areas, then fully fold and stick down the flaps in the order indicated—and there is your envelope. The last flap can be tucked inside the envelope after the card is inserted—or you can stick it down if you prefer.

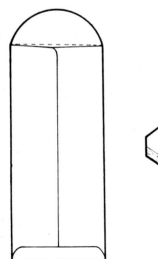

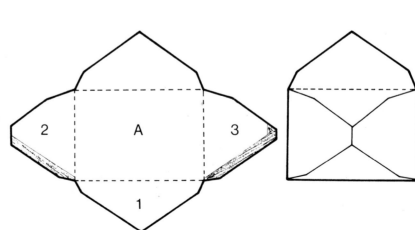

Other ways to use the techniques

One of the most imaginative and encouraging aspects of modern design has been the combination of existing, traditional patterns and styles with new media. Our homes and personal possessions have been transformed—sheets bloom with Monet's waterlilies or colonial wallpaper bouquets, cushions are covered with needlepoint patchwork quilts or embroidered Chinese plates, and tee-shirts become walking posters for Coca-Cola or the latest hit record. The designs in this book are equally adaptable—the only limitations are those of your own imagination.

One of the easiest and most satisfying crafts is stencil work, and the chapter beginning on page 19 tells you how to make and use stencil designs. Once you have the knack of using stencils, the possibilities are enormous. For instance —to begin with, you could finish off painted or plain-papered walls with stencil borders. For a small room, stencils made for the cards would probably be big enough, and for a bathroom or dressing area the butterfly design on page 22 would be delightful in colours which pick up the tones of your carpet and tiles. Check with your paint shop about the right product (if you are working on tiles, for example, you will need oil-based paints). The butterflies could go around the top of the walls as a frieze, frame the doors and windows, and even, in a miniature version, make a setting for doorknobs or cabinet locks to match. If your walls are completely tiled in a background colour, adjust the stencil size to the individual tile, and make an all-over pattern on every other tile, or scattered in natural clusters on the walls. If you haven't done this before, it's a good idea to cut out a number of butterfly shapes in ordinary coloured paper (don't bother about the inside, just make simple outlines) and stick up with double-sided adhesive tape where you think you would like them to go. This will give you a good idea of balance and spacing, and will improve the finished result enormously. For papered or emulsioned areas, use one of the proprietary putty-like adhesives made for the purpose, and you'll be able to change the spacing and position easily without damaging the surface.

If your pattern is to be all of one colour, then one stencil should be enough—use it until the edges begin to get a little battered from the paint roller or stencil brush. But if you are planning to have a multi-coloured stencil, it will be necessary to make separate stencils for the different colours.

Make pinholes at the extremities of the pattern on the stencil for each colour; these can be positioned accurately, so that each colour is stencilled down in exactly the right place, one on another. In the case of the butterfly, the first stencil would have only the outline of the body, wings and antennae cut into it; use this first with your basic colour (black or brown, for example) which will establish the form of your border along the wall. Use a small roller and non-drip paint, lifting the stencil carefully each time and moving over to the next space. In this way the entire layout can be achieved without having to wait for each unit to dry. The next stencil should have cut-outs only for the next strongest colour —perhaps the pattern of forewings and eye spots on the back wings. The pinholes at the outer edges of the design will let you position the stencil in the right place. Go along the row with your red paint, being careful not to pick up too much or it will run down the wall. This is more likely to happen on a wall than when making cards, so try out a few on a practice board, or somewhere where a mess doesn't matter, to make sure you have the right load on your brush or roller. Better too little than too much, as you can always go over it again. After the red has dried, finish off with the two highlight colours, pink and green, or whatever colours you've chosen, always remembering to check that the pinholes line up in the same place each time you put the stencil down.

Designs can be adapted to stencils, and stencils adapted for use in almost every situation; blow up some of the smaller patterns for wall and floor use (remember to coat the floor afterwards with two or three coats of clear polyurethane varnish to protect your painted pattern) or reduce for furniture and other woodwork projects. Small tables are particularly suitable for stencils enlarged to cover part or all of the top, and even secondary stencils on the legs. Furniture can be painted with almost anything from delicate floral and gilt designs on the back rails of chairs (windsor and hitch-cock chairs are traditionally decorated in this way) to bold, modern patterns which cover a whole set of small sidetables. In general, the more complicated designs are most effective when enlarged, but there are always the exceptions, and a very simple pattern in brilliant colours can add enormous 'lift' to any room.

Many of the smaller patterns, cut-outs or traced designs can be used to decorate dolls' houses and doll furniture. A pattern made from the frame design on page 63 would make a lovely painted carpet for a doll's living room or, reduced

Opposite: Why not use the techniques you have learnt in making your own table and party decorations?

even further and painted on the wall, a frame for a mirror or reproduction painting cut from a magazine. Potato-cut prints, using a small, simple pattern, can make excellent wallpaper sheets for the rooms.

Embroidery is another good use for many of the card designs, and it can be used in two ways. The patterns themselves can be adapted to needlepoint or crewel work—the traced pattern of flowers would make a brilliant cushion or set of chair seats; and the alphabet or number designs which are done on graph paper can be used for tent-stitch needlepoint very easily—just count the spaces, one to each stitch, as you would a graphed pattern in an embroidery book. You could use almost any of the designs as patterns to be traced onto canvas or linen or felt, and embroidered in any style that pleases you, and in any colour.

The designs and techniques and materials we have described can all be used for the creation of table and party decorations, which are all the more exciting when you have made them yourself. We have illustrated a few on page 105. Paper of every colour and finish can be used to make cut-out chains of doves touching wings endlessly across the room. Paper or card lanterns give ordinary electric light a mysterious and glowing quality, and many of the designs we have shown would look splendid cut out in this way. Choose your colours with care—remember that blues give a cool, underwater light, pinks and reds are warm and cheerful and generally flattering, but greens can make the healthiest tennis-club champion look ready for the next ambulance. The simplest ideas can be very decorative, such as the ornamental flower in the photograph, made from cards of different colours, cut out, bent forward and glued together. Blots, cut-outs and collages can be applied to the most basic boxes and containers—whether in the study, the bathroom, the bedroom or the kitchen. Even the humble egg can be turned into a festive decoration for table or tree—or simply hung on a piece of cotton. The three eggs in the photograph have been painted with silver, blues, greens, and reds, and look very effective. Patience and care in painting the designs, even simple ones, is amply rewarded.

The cards themselves can be mounted and either sent as small gifts or made into pictures. For Christmas-tree ornaments, which have become so popular recently, take one of the star or Easter-egg patterns and lay it out on whatever fabric you choose. Pencil outline two shapes for each ornament, touching at one point. Embroider the designs in whatever form you have chosen, then cut around the double pattern, leaving a small hem beyond the pencil line. Sew together, starting each side from the base where the two halves are connected, using an overcase stitch in a bright wool. The easiest method is to sew along the right side, merely folding the hem in as you go; but for thin fabrics, sew together on the wrong side as usual, along the pencil line, leaving enough space at the top to turn the entire ornament inside out before stuffing with cotton or plastic foam. In either case, stitch the two halves together firmly on top, finishing off with a ribbon or gold-wire loop to hang on the tree.

Other ornaments can be made from the fish or cat designs, and a whole set in different colours and trimmings can be amusing and very easy for children to do. Cut out the basic pattern from felt in as many bright colours as you can find. For a very sophisticated look, stick to one colour such as yellow or white, and keep the trimmings to similar tones, but in a variety of materials and textures. Follow the basic instructions for the other patterns by laying out the double card design, leaving the two connected at the bottom, or at one end. If you are embroidering the design, do that while the fabric is flat. You can vary the expression on the cat's face considerably by changing his smile and his eyes. For very young children, pencil the basic outlines in; but half their fun will come from designing their own decorations. Then stick on sequins or fancy buttons wherever you choose. Cut out the design as indicated, sew up, stuff, and cover the seams with a length of gold or tinsel ribbon that is long enough to go around the seam completely, and leave enough at the top for a loop, and a bow. Of course, this method could also be used on a larger scale to make the soft toys that teenagers love so much, and the only limit on the filling pattern is their time and patience.

Children can also make themselves stunning room decorations by building up a collage from a number of suitable designs. The effect can be adapted to any space or style you choose. The important thing is to have enough of them in all sorts of colours to really make an impact. A decoration for a nursery or a young person's literary room can be made more dreamy and romantic as a mural, using a number of the silhouette designs. A very young child would need a little more help in enlarging or reducing some of the designs so that their sizes are in balance with each other, but all the ingredients of a fairy-tale landscape are there—a castle on the hill, a house below in a valley with trees, streams, a lake with a sailing boat, and horses in the paddock—you could easily cover a whole wall. Keep the silhouettes black against a pale, contrasting colour.

For the woodworker or carpenter who wants to make something extra-special another trick is to use the lino-cut patterns in reverse; instead of cutting them into lino-blocks for use as printing bases, cut into soft wood (or even balsa wood for beginners), stain in traditional wood tones or some of the newer Scandinavian-type colours, and use the wood-blocks for lamp bases, tops of cigarette boxes, card boxes, or even inlaid into table tops. Adjust the design to the basic shape you want, of course, and use a wood suitable for the project—pine or deal for woodblocks and box-tops, thinner balsa wood for lighter objects like note-book covers or mirror frames. You can even adapt the tree design on page 70, for instance, for the edge of a wooden salad bowl, which you can buy undecorated, and preferably unstained. These are often sold in kitchen departments and wood supply shops. After you have cut the design round the surface, stain the entire bowl, and you will have a unique and beautiful piece of real craftsmanship.

Simple designs can also be used in fabric painting and dyeing; follow directions for batik printing in a speciality book and use stencils as directed. For matching table sets, take a design like the chrysanthemum.

There are new fabric and china paints available which can be used on plain, white plates and ready-made tablemats. Paint the motif on the rim of the plate, with a matching motif on a tablemat and napkin. Make as many sets as you need place settings.

A different effect can be achieved by using blot designs in glowing fluorescent colours, just as described on page 75. Buy a set of simple, clear perspex or lucite tablemats, and make your blots on pieces of paper of the same size and shape which are then glued carefully underneath the mats. A film of thin plastic glued to the back of the paper will give added protection from the surface of the table. This method is particularly effective on clear-glass tabletops when the light from below shines through the design. Similar effects can be gained using clear lucite boxes and accessories.

Books to read

Banister, M. *Prints from Linoblocks and Woodcuts.* New York 1967; London 1968.

Bentley, W. A., and Humphreys, W. .J. *Snow Crystals.* New York and London 1963.

Binder, P. *Magic Symbols of the World.* London 1972.

Bowles and Carrer. *Catchpenny Prints. 163 Popular Engravings from the Eighteenth Century.* New York and London 1970.

Chapman, S. E. *Early American Design Motifs.* New York 1974; London 1975.

D'Arbeloff, N., and Yates, J. *Creating in Collage.* London 1971.

Domnitz, M. *Judaism.* London 1970.

Enciso, J. *Design Motifs of Ancient Mexico.* New York 1947; London 1958.

Field, F. V. *Pre-Hispanic Mexican Stamp Design Motifs.* New York 1974; London 1975.

Gillon, E. V., Jr. *Decorative Borders and Frames: 395 Examples from the Renaissance to the Present Day.* New York and London 1973.

Gillon, E. V., Jr. *Picture Sourcebook for Collage and Decoupage.* New York 1974; London 1975.

Gillon, E. V., Jr. *Victorian Stencils for Design and Decoration.* New York 1968; London 1969.

Glass, F. J. *Stencil Craft.* Novato, Ca. 1971

Hornung, C. P. *Handbook of Designs and Devices.* New York 1946; London 1958.

Laliberte, N., and Mogelon, A. *Art of Stencil: History and Modern Uses.* New York 1971; London 1972.

Laliberte, N., and Mogelon, A. *Collage, Montage, Assemblage.* New York and London 1972.

Menken, T. *The Art Deco Style in Household Objects, Architecture, Scultpure, Graphics, Jewelry.* New York 1972; London 1973.

Menken, T., *Art Nouveau and Early Art Deco Type and Design.* New York 1972; London 1973.

Paterson, G. W. L. *Making a Colour Linocut.* Leicester 1963.

Simister, W. *How to Use Scraperboard.* Newton Abbot 1971.
Simister, W. *How to Use Scratchboard.* New York 1972.
Simms, C., and Simms, G. *Introducing Seed Collage.* London 1971.
Strose, S. *Potato Printing.* New York 1968; London 1969.
Tuer, A. W. *Japanese Stencil Designs.* New York and London 1968.

Index